Missy's Clan – Deer Friends

True cat stories with wonderful pictures.

Cristina Berna and Eric Thomsen

2024

Missy's Clan – Deer Friends

True cat stories with wonderful pictures.

Cristina Berna and Eric Thomsen

ISBN US 978-0-2712-7706-6

This title is available in color print in the United States under ISBN 978-1-3830-0958-3

About the authors

Cristina Berna loves photographing and writing. She also creates designs and advice on fashion and styling.

Eric Thomsen has published in science, economics and law, created exhibitions and arranged concerts.

Also by the authors:

World of Cakes

Luxembourg – a piece of cake

Florida Cakes

Catalan Pastis – Catalonian Cakes

Andalucian Delight

World of Art

Hokusai – 36 Views of Mt Fuji

Christmas Nativity

Christmas Nativity – Spain

Christmas Nativities Luxembourg Trier

Christmas Nativity United States

Christmas Nativity Hallstatt

Christmas Markets

Christmas Market Innsbruck

Christmas Market Vienna

Christmas Market Slovenia

Outpets

Deer in Dyrehaven – Outpets in Denmark

Florida Outpets

Birds of Play

Missy's Clan

Missy's Clan – The Beginning

Missy's Clan – Christmas

Missy's Clan – Education

Missy's Clan – Kittens

Missy's Clan – Deer Friends

Missy's Clan – Outpets

Missy's Clan – Outpet Birds

Vehicles

Copenhagen vehicles – and a trip to Sweden

Construction vehicles picture book

Trains

American Police Cars

Contact the authors

missysclan@gmail.com

Published by www.missysclan.net

Cover picture: Newborn fawn at the plot called Kansas

Inside: Cottonball on the look-out

Missy's Clan – Deer Friends

If you have read "Missy´s Clan *The Beginning*" or some of the other titles you will already be familiar with some of Missy's Clan.

Missy was an orphan kitten, who befriended Cristina.

Anjuli and Minnie were two of her daughters. Their father was Big-Tiger – a huge and handsome ginger Bachelor, who was the king of the King's Road.

He crossed this road daily which had a traffic of 40.000 cars and one day we saw him no more.

- Uhmm, *Ilex* leaves are very tasty!

No, it is not a spelling error. It is not "Dear" friends but "Deer" friends...as in Roe deer – Buck, Roe and Fawn.

Actually, they were not *"dear"* at all the first time!

Right here Anjuli and Lille-Tiger saw two deer the first time. Their eyes widened, hair stuck out, tails all bottle cleaner brush like. The deer jumped them and galloped down the bridge and disappeared into the Orchard, down a steep slope to the left and the end of the bridge. Shed No 1 to the left, which Anjuli loved.

Eric was on the porch by the back entrance, reading in the sunlight, and Anjuli and Lille-Tiger were guarding the entrance to the bridge.

It was under this wooden bridge Missy had her first litter (see *"Beginning"*).

Suddenly there was a commotion.

When excited the cat's tail would look like a brush to clean bottles with.

Lille-Tiger had a tail like a fox and his hair stood straight out 90 degrees from the skin, all over his body. Eyes glowing terrified!

Anjuli was in defense mode, sunken halfway into the ground and growling like a real tiger, bolts flashing from her eyes.

Two roe deer had come from the garden, past Shed no 1, and were walking towards the cats.

The deer had not seen Eric, on the porch by the Bird House, behind the board barriers.

The explosion of sounds with the frightened cats scared the deer, who sprang over the cats, galloped along

The deer had come down this "road" from the lawn down to Shed No 1, which is just out of the picture to the right. This is the deer on another occasion, pictured through the living room window.

the wooden bridge, past Eric, jumped the gate at the end and disappeared down the slope into the Orchard, past the neighbor's bird shed.

- Mmmm, lovely weed, this – Midsummer Herb (*Hylotelephium*).

Eric went to comfort the cats.

- Did you *see that?* Anjuli's eyes enquired. They were *huge!* I never saw such big animals before, right here in

our garden! Lille-Tiger's eyes were like
– What were those *creatures?*

It took some time before the cats
calmed down.

Deer roaming the front lawn by the Cat Climbing Tree and the
clothes drying line. Magpie to the right. Picture taken from a
window on the first floor.

After this first encounter we were to have deer permanently in the garden.

When the deer first discovered the garden with all its grass lawns and various plants in spring time they installed themselves on a permanent basis.

Usually they would trek past The Pavilion from the neighboring plot, which was a wild birch and willow wood growing on municipal land. This plot had been planned for a big school catering to the adjacent municipal housing estates. Budget constraints changed the plans.

We imagined these housing estates as a distant (although sometimes very noisy) mountain ridge that could be seen through the trees in the Orchard and along the shores of the lake. Put a sort of distance to the reality.

The Lake seen from the path past The Pavilion by Anjuli's look out tower. You can just glimpse the housing estates as a distant mountain range. Sometimes kids would scale the fence and play on the ice, but luckily no one ever drowned.

The wood covering the municipal plot was to the one side of the ring road around the city. To the other side were industrial areas and fields, which connected to large acreage of forest and plantation, with lots of deer and other wildlife.

It is interesting how the animals will recapture land from where they have been driven, as soon as human activity decreases enough. Or will recapture it even when humans are still there.

The deer brought a worry, though.

They are accused of carrying ticks that can transfer a terrible disease –

One of the artificial lakes in the woods above Yoda's village, built to store water for the iron smithy water mill. Today a popular recreational area with lots of wildlife.

Borelia. Recent research appeared to claim that the ticks were carried on mice and not deer.

This made us weary of being bare footed or have too much skin contact

Upper Kansas plot where the deer often assembled to the right in some bushes and high grass

with the grass. We always used a rug when playing with the cats.

The cats often had ticks.

You would discover them when the cats came to be stroked.

Then we started the tick procedure.

Take a piece of paper tissue.

Apply white spirits, to get the tick drunk.

Lower Kansas plot ending in a slope up to the King's Road. The deer would flee left through the hedge to the front lawn. The thorn hedge is almost invisible, covered by a row of hazel trees lowed by squirrels.

Apply the tissue around the tick, grab around the tick with the spirit soaked tissue and keep moving the tick in small circles.

Whether drunk or annoyed by the movement the tick would invariably let go and we could flush it in the toilet.

You have to be careful not to pull and break the tick. Then you would have a sack of blood in your fingers and the head of the tick would still be lodged in the skin of the cat, and would be impossible to remove.

It would grow out again and you would have to wait for it to be big enough to have another try at removing it.

Fleeing deer on the front lawn, Red House in the back ground, Kansas shed to the right (which served as covered kitten playground for a while).

The cats, however, hated the procedure, perhaps because the spirits irritated their delicate sense of smell. However, they appreciated the ticks were gone.

Fawn in the high grass on the Kansas plot.

Several years the deer had fawns if we let some strips grow to high grass. There was a piece of the Kansas plot which was difficult to mow with the small hand mower. We used up a new hand mower every year, it was tough work.

The little fawn would be abandoned when Eric came with the mower to clear the path to The Red House and at least some of the Kansas plot by the sheds.

Mother Roe would dart through the hedge by the Hazelnut Trees and watch scared from the front lawn.

The little fawn would lie completely still, even with this terrible creature of a mower making such a noise and threatening to cut the fawn to pieces!

Mother Roe must have thought the mower a vicious animal, with all that noise. Eric would also have preferred the mower to be a bit more quiet!

Another year a roe had a fawn down in the Orchard, almost below the house.

The Orchard was a small low piece of land, we planted with apples, pears and prunes.

It bordered the lake to one side, had an entrance to the vast grass lawns of the housing estate in the horizon and to the back yards of three neighbors on the third side.

Our house and main garden was on a big clay knoll. The lake was actually a clay excavation which had been abandoned and filled with water.

Rumors had it there was a complete train at the bottom of the lake. Now it was filled with fish, various types of frog and salamanders. It was a great miniature Nature Reserve with a huge number of frogs passing the house every Spring.

Roe on the front lawn by an old double Lilac tree, Kansas plot on the other side of the hedge, pear tree to the right in which the kittens laved to climb, Ilex front left.

A heron used to come in for a daily landing, circling many times and he completed the difficult landing between the tall trees. Looked like a plane landing in a difficult high altitude airfield between the mountains.

Roe by the large *Rhododendrum* bush by the old Bike Shed (where Anjuli hid her kittens one year).

It was funny to watch the group of deer when they were at peace over by Kansas. Often they would be staring out on the King's Road with the heavy traffic.

You could see them wonder about these animals which roared past on the big path on the other side of the low stone wall.

It looked as if they were watching television.

Both the cats and we got on well with the deer when we had accustomed ourselves to them. They were happy to let us be as long as they could access the vegetation for food and have shelter. Friendly neighbors!

Roe on the front lawn quite close to the garden door of the living room. She had spotted the photographer in the main entrance doorway.

We tried slowly to tame them, to make them into *outpets*. (see "Missy's Clan *Outpets*").

Cottonball would object to too much picture taking and friendly sounds, because this was an activity reserved for *family*. Too much picture taking signified an interest which not according to proper form, and she would interpose herself.

Cottonball interposing herself on a photo shoot of the deer. Too much picture taking of *outpets* revealed an unhealthy interest not accorded to such lowly status. Only *family* could have their pictures freely taken.

We did not get so far as to be feeding the deer, but we had this wild plan of buying a cattle salt stone for them to lick – and to tame them by making them more used to us this way.

Roe happily ignorant of status conflicts. Considers herself *prey* and not *outpet* at this level of intimacy.

You might argue this was not really fair to the deer.

The Prince and his court hunted the deer out in the woods and if they became too accustomed to us, they might walk right into the killing.

Even though the thought might have occurred to our cats we did not hunt the deer.

It would have been easy enough, but we enjoyed so much to have these beautiful friends around in the garden to look at.

You don't have to kill every animal you see!

Roe in the *Forsythia* bushes up to the thorn hedge between the Front Lawn and Kansas. A hide out.

One winter there were seven young deer residing under the trees at the end of the office wing, by the Juniper Tree where the Magpie Kid was almost killed by Lille-Maske (see "Missy´s Clan *Outpet Birds*").

Roe eating the Ilex bush, captured through the garden door in the living room. The spot where the kittens used to play in summer time.

- Now they are looking again!

The young deer would feed on the various bushes and the remaining, mostly dried, grass.

The garden food must have been very delicate and tasty, because there is plenty of food out in the woods and as such no need to come into the garden.

In the summer there would not be as many deer in the garden as in the wintertime. This point to the availability of delicate food as the reason.

The density of roe in the woods here was also not of a level to force them to seek our garden in the city. So why this big flock of young deer stayed with us in the garden is interesting.

Deer by the hedge to Kansas.

Whenever Eric had to go down and take the train, he would walk that way past the flock of deer – and stop and talk to them.

They were curious and did not flee – as long as Eric kept a certain distance.

Deer on the front lawn

But come closer than that – and the deer would scramble over the hedge to the neighbor's lawn and flee between the houses, which were usually unoccupied in the daytime. Nobody home to shoot them up.

It's a sort of wealthy feeling to have "your own" deer in your garden in the city!

Like an Indian Maharaja!

Deer pictured from the garden door only a few meters away.

We never saw them approach the King's Road – not even when they fled. They appeared very conscious of the road traffic as dangerous if interfered with. No need for a sign with a jumping deer!

Often the deer would be right outside, by the garden door of the living room, where the cats played with the kittens in summertime.

They appeared to have become used to our cats, but neither sought the company of the other species.

Our cats kept a healthy distance of these big animals but after the initial scare, apart from protesting about the

Ok, close enough! Don't bother me! I'll be leaving this party!

increasing familiarity of *outpet* status, they did not object.

There was an incident with two stray dogs that entered our garden and chased the deer.

The owners had them unleashed on the footpath past the south end of the garden.

When they scented the deer in the garden, the owners lost all control, and the dogs came barking in big leaps

The path past Shed No 2 up to The Pavilion, where the deer entered from the municipal plot.

through the hedge, over the lawn and into Kansas.

We happened to be at the circle where the great tits nested.

The deer exploded out of Kansas, over the lawn and up past The Pavilion into the woods.

We called out to the dogs, but they just showed happy oblivious faces with tongues dangling.

The dogs' owners did not take kindly to admonishments of keeping their dogs under control, even when unleashed. Some dog owners have an attitude and "trespass" has no meaning to them. They start to yell at you and insult you.

Spring again – the *Rhododendrum* on the front lawn, with the Old Walnut behind. We will tell you about the squirrels and the walnuts in another issue.

Luckily there were no small fawns to be killed by the dogs at that time.

The state decided to improve the King's Road and all the noise from the heavy equipment and activity from the workers scared the deer, and unfortunately they moved out.

After that it was only in wintertime the deer came occasionally to forage.

We miss them very much!

Deer by the hedge to Kansas

Let us look at some other people´s pictures.

A childhood memory is of the family dog – a Collie – chasing the cats, just for fun and never touching them.

But she had great fun making them run into the barn where they disappeared and she let it go.

The animosity between cats and dogs is an old story.

Just look at this picture.

This is from a base of a funerary kouros for the grave of an athlete, executed in pentelic marble. It is in Athens, Kerameikos and is built into the Themistokleian wall which is from 510 BC.

Here is a completely different story.

This is a picture of deep love.

Sleeping on top of a warm mattress – you could call it a hot dog, right? – is so wonderful.

The owner behind this pictures explains that the two Balinese cats – long-haired Siamese cats and two miniature Dachshounds – grew up together and that is why they got on so well together.

The same story is heard again and again from people with both dogs and cats.

Here is a wonderful picture showing what the owner was talking about – whelp and kitten growing up together.

Note the use of old newspaper to catch any "mishaps".

Love between dogs and cats can run even deeper.

Here is a dog suckling two kittens and they are clearly growing well.

The word for a female dog is "bitch" but this word is often also used as a derogative.

A dog and a cat at a countryside cottage writes this owner.

The cat is keeping the chained dog company.

The cat is allowed to roam freely but it mostly stays at home with her friend.

Even more cosy and friendly is this pair.

The cat is sharing the dog house with the dog and both exude the expression "best of friends" – both saying "we are comfortable, thank you".

Here is another lovely picture of a cat and a Yorkshire Terrier being the best of friends. Note the absolutely hilarious expression the kitten has – what are you doing? We have seen this expression so many times when you fish out the camera.

Ōide Tōkō (1841–1905) - cat watching a spider, Japanese Album leaf; ink and color on silk, The Metropolitan Museum of Art.

Cats have a natural instinct to hunt, and those eight-legged creatures are just too tempting to resist.

Most cats enjoy a game of chase when they spot a spider. Although cats won't eliminate an entire infestation, they will help get rid of the odd few around the house.

Sometimes a cat will bring you a half-dead spider – our mouse or rat if you have them – as a gift and as evidence that they are keeping the contract with humans of taking care of these unwanted animals in return for food and shelter.

Most spiders are not dangerous to cats.

In Norse mythology, the goddess Freyja was associated with cats. Farmers sought protection for their crops by leaving pans of milk in their fields for Freya's special feline companions, the two grey cats who fought with her and pulled her chariot.

Another popular Nordic folklore figure is the "Nisse" – a household spirit engaged in various household and stable chores and expected to be rewarded at least once a year at solstice with porridge.

A nisse is a small human like figure with a red hat who today has merged to become Santa´s Helpers.

These small fellows would of course be well known to the cats on the farm, as they are able to go the same places due to their size.

There are many tales about what the nisse could do to trouble you if you upset them and failed to honor them.

Therefore, the giving of milk and porridge, usually out in the stables was like an insurance policy in order to ward off the wrath of these small fellows. Maybe the cat drank the milk.

In a book of fairy tales from 1884 a Danish artist has shown how he imagines the nisse looks like and how one of them is talking to a cat.

Erik Werenskiold (1855–1938): Nisse and ca, 1884.

Above is the illustration from the fairytale book by Danish editor Asbjørnsen, Peter Christen , ed. (1884) *Eventyrbog for Børn*, Kjøbenhavn: Gyldendal, translates to Fairytale Book for Children.

There is a saying in Danish that "Nissen flytter med" – the nisse moves with you to your new house or farm.

The deeper meaning of this is that you have to deal with your problems – you can´t just move to somewhere else and escape the problems, especially if the problems are of your own doing.

The meaning is that you have to change your own habits.

Jan Baptist Weenix (1621–circa 1660) A Dog and a Cat near a partially disembowelled Deer   between circa 1647 and circa 1660 height: 180 cm (70.8 in) ; width: 162 cm (63.7 in) Rijksmuseum Amsterdam.

A hunter has been disturbed by a phone call or something and has left his work of disemboweling a deer he has hunted over in the woods.

In those days it was normal to slaughter and prepare meat at home, where today all that is done away from the house and you just go to the supermarket and buy meat ready packed.

Out cats were deeply impressed by this system – they wanted to come along and see how we hunted and how we prepared the meat in these neat portions, all minced and chopped. They would have been deeply disappointed to learn the truth.

Unknown artist A Brown Horse in a Stable with a Cat and a Mouse   between 1800 and 1899   height: 43 cm (16.9 in); width: 56 cm (22 in) National Trust

A cat engaged in fulfillment of the contract with humans.

This grey cat is chasing a mouse in the horse box and the horse is unperturbed.

These animals are small and pose no threat to a horse. The horse is afraid of larger cats like lions and tigers that were the real danger where the horses lived as wild.

That is why, sometimes, a horse gets scared of the rider on its back – instinctively the horse shuts down its thinking and just tries to run away from the predator that is trying to bring it down, has jumped on its back and sunk its teeth in its neck. This is a standard hunting technique of the big cats and which you can see in safari films.

If you don´t fall off you must talk and pat the horse while you hang on there.

Aelbert Cuyp (1620–1691): Kicking Horse, 1645 and 1649, Philadelphia Museum of Art.

It is different with dogs. They have a size that can be dangerous to horses, especially if the dogs hunt in packs.

Here is a painting with a dog annoying a horse with its barking.

George Stubbs (1724–1806): Horse Frightened by a Lion,
between 1762 and 1768, Yale Center of British Art

While horses and cats get on very well,
often forming great friendships, it is
different with the big cats.

It is all about size.

The world is a dangerous place.

Antoine-Louis Barye (1795 - 1875): Horse Attacked by a Tiger, bronze, model 1837 or before, cast possibly after 1875, size overall: 26.1 x 36.9 x 16.2 cm (10 1/4 x 14 1/2 x 6 3/8 in.), Collection of Mr. and Mrs. Paul Mellon, National Museum of Art, Washington, D.C.

A beautiful small statue of a tiger jumping on the horse´s back and sinking its teeth it´s neck.

Deer in Dyrehaven

Dyrehaven North of Copenhagen offers fantastic opportunities to enjoy the sight of deer - and it is absolutely FREE! Dyrehaven was originally established as a royal hunting ground. Dyrehaven is also home to the World's oldest ongoing amusement park – BAKKEN. This amusement park has many rides, restaurants, ice cream shops and a traditional variety of food stalls and restaurants. *Deer in Dyrehaven* is filled with the author's own pictures.

ISBN 978-2-621-816-963

” As the afternoon wears on, careful advance parties will emerge from the dark of the forest – observing if any wolves are nearby - and then sprint out into the open grassland.

When they are far enough out on the plain, they will stop and start grazing – or join herds already so engaged.

You will see a "sentry" deer keeping watch".

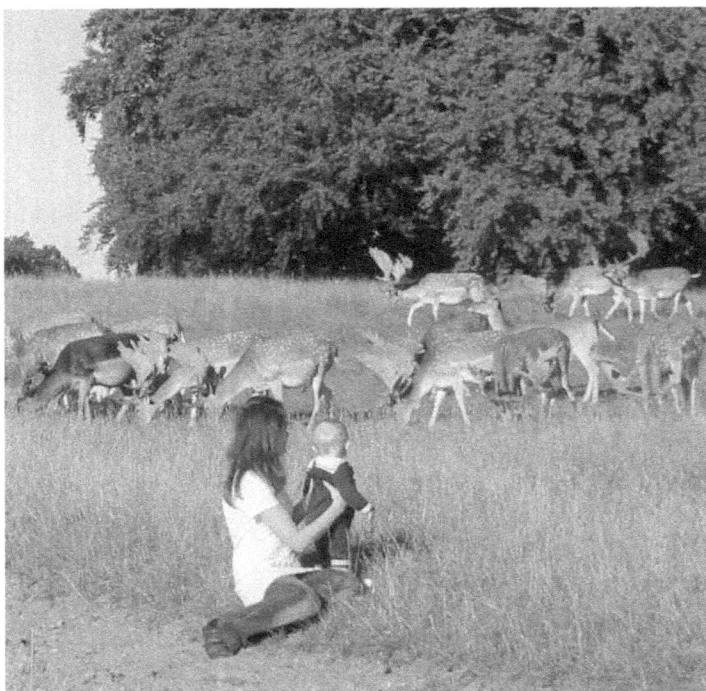

Male fallow deer (*Dama dama*) - bucks - in Danish: Dådyr - grazing on the Plain of the Eremitage near the small hunting lodge called the Eremitage – remember to keep your distance. ©Berna 2016.

The fallow buck drops the antlers in May-June, and brush the new set in August-September, brush the skin which carried blood vessels with nutrition to the antlers away so the horn-calcium antlers are ready for the parade at the right time.